EMPOWERING
MOMENTS
VOL. II

EMPOWERING MOMENTS
VOL. II

30 Day Devotional

SHAVON SELLERS

Copyright © 2019 Shavon Sellers.

All rights reserved. No part of this publication may be reproduced, distributed, or transmitted in any form or by any means, including photocopying, recording, or other electronic or mechanical methods, without the prior written permission of the publisher, except in the case of brief quotations embodied in critical reviews and certain other noncommercial uses permitted by copyright law. For permission requests, write to the publisher, addressed "Attention: Permissions Coordinator," at the address below.

ISBN: 978-1-7341479-5-7 (Paperback)
978-1-7341479-6-4 (E-Book)

Library of Congress Control Number: 2019957805

Front cover image by Prize Publishing House, LLC.
Book design by Prize Publishing House, LLC.

Printed by Prize Publishing House, LLC, in the United States of America.

First printing edition 2020.

Prize Publishing House
P.O. Box 9856
Chesapeake, VA 23321

www.PrizePublishingHouse.com

Contents

INTRODUCTION VII

DAY 1   A NECESSARY EVIL 1

DAY 2   GOD HAS NOT FORGOT 5

DAY 3   ENLARGE MY TERRITORY 8

DAY 4   IT'S AN INSIDE JOB 11

DAY 5   I SHALL LIVE AND NOT DIE 14

DAY 6   GODLY CONFIDENCE 17

DAY 7   IT'S ALREADY DONE 20

DAY 8   ALL THINGS ARE POSSIBLE 23

DAY 9   NEVER FORSAKEN 26

DAY 10   GOD'S PLAN 29

DAY 11   I'M GOOD AT THE GATE 32

DAY 12   BE THE LIGHT 35

DAY 13   GIANTS DO FALL 38

DAY 14	I AM READY FOR OVERFLOW	41
DAY 15	I BELONG HERE	44
DAY 16	IT CANNOT BE DENIED	47
DAY 17	COMMAND IT	50
DAY 18	DIG DEEPER	53
DAY 19	NO MORE MISSED SEASONS	56
DAY 20	SET BACK FOR A SETUP	59
DAY 21	TRANSFORMED BY HIS GLORY	62
DAY 22	I AM WHAT YOU SEE	66
DAY 23	THE FIGHT IS FIXED	69
DAY 24	FAITH – FORSAKING ALL I TRUST HIM	72
DAY 25	ACCESS GRANTED	76
DAY 26	BE BOLD – JUST DO IT!!	79
DAY 27	NOT GUILTY	82
DAY 28	REAL LOVE	85
DAY 29	THE POWER OF PATIENCE	88
DAY 30	A HEART TO WORSHIP	92

Introduction

Maintaining a relationship with Christ requires commitment, dedication, and a desire to become closer to Him. One way to grow closer in your relationship with God is to spend quiet time alone with Him each day. Your faith in Jesus Christ is a daily walk; therefore, you must pray continually and spend time with Him to ensure your faith never waivers. You must be strengthened daily.

There are several ways to spend time with God, one of which is daily devotion. It is my prayer that you will remain humble, committed, and steadfast as you go on this 30-day journey. May you grow closer to God and may you grow into a better understanding of who He is to you. Daily scripture reading is essential to your growth and provides guidance for your next step of faith.

Devotion is also a form of worship. When you can quiet yourself and think about who and what God is to you, you are able to worship Him more freely. You are able to reflect on your relationship and areas of growth. God desires a relationship with you. Just like you are intentional and expend great effort to get to know someone, God requires the same effort. He requires your time. He requires your energy. He requires your love and attention. A key component of all relationships is intimacy, which requires time spent together and getting to know each other.

Surrender your will to God. Talk to Him about the details of your day. Seek direction. Learn His truth and gain wisdom and understanding. When you have done this and spend time in devotion, you will grow to know and understand the voice of God. You will know when He is speaking to you and you will know when the voice may be that of the adversary. You will begin to better understand His promises and the plans that He has for your life.

As you read this devotional, I pray that your walk with Christ and your faith is strengthened. Be intentional. Start each day with prayer. Reflect on your spiritual growth. Take the time to step away from your daily routine and feed your spirit. Quiet time is essential to your walk. May this devotional be a blessing to you and may you be renewed on this journey!!

Day 1

A NECESSARY EVIL

2 Corinthians 12:9-10 (KJV)

***9** And he said unto me, "My grace is sufficient for thee: for my strength is made perfect in weakness". Most gladly therefore will I rather glory in my infirmities, that the power of Christ may rest upon me. **10** Therefore I take pleasure in infirmities, in reproaches, in necessities, in persecutions, in distresses for Christ's sake: for when I am weak, then am I strong.*

Whether your journey with Christ is fairly new or you have been in relationship with Him for decades, you may have come to realize that it is not always easy. As a matter of fact, life may seem much harder since you began living for Christ; your marriage seems to be falling apart, there is more money leaving your bank account than there is going in, repossession notices are coming in, loved ones are suffering in abuse, or problems at your job. This list can probably go on and on and you may find yourself asking God the big question of "WHY?" You are living right, you are reading your

Bible daily, you are at church for bible study and Sunday morning worship, you are the one that gives to others when they are in need, you are the one that turns the other cheek when people do you wrong; and yet, you still can't seem to catch a break. You didn't seem to have all these problems when you were in the world living with no worries about sin, so why now God?

The Apostle Paul had the same concern and asked the similar question. Before he was Paul, he was Saul, and Saul was a man that was eager to kill those who followed Christ and robbed the churches. He desired to have absolutely nothing to do with Jesus or Jesus' followers until he had a major encounter with Jesus on the Damascus Road when Jesus asked, "Saul! Saul! Why are you persecutest thou me?" (Acts 9:4) That initial encounter led to Saul becoming Paul and he became one of the most profound followers of Christ and dedicated the rest of his life telling people about the love of Jesus Christ. But it was not until he began preaching the gospel of Jesus Christ that he began to suffer greatly. Paul was beaten and thrown in prison, stoned, flogged, shipwrecked, all for the cause of Christ. And just like you, Paul wanted to know 'Why?' The Apostle Paul asked the Lord to remove his thorn, those things that were sent to torment and hurt him; as a matter of fact, Paul asked three times. But the Lord's reply was "My grace is all you need. My power works best in weakness." (2 Corinthians 12:8-9)

Just as God's grace was all that Paul needed, His grace is all that you need as well. Your thorns, those hurts that you are praying to God about, are there because God wants you to continue to seek Him for strength. It is in our weak moments, our trials, when God can show the world why He is God. That thorn is there to remind you that it is He that will change your situation, all that is required of you is

FAITH in Him to do so. Worrying, fear, and doubt are all signs that there is a lack of faith, but when you can rejoice even in your times of weakness, hurt, anguish, disappointments and know that God is working it all out in your favor, that shows STRENGTH. Paul said it best, "…For when I am weak, then I am strong." (2 Corinthians 12:10)

~My Prayer~

Father God, I want to thank You for helping me to see that even in the midst of my hurt, my pain, chaotic moments, Your grace is always with me. It is because of Your grace that I can wear my thorn with gladness knowing that no matter what it looks like around me, You are my strength; and in knowing that, I can endure. God, I thank You for showing me that it is all NECESSARY; it's necessary for my faith, growth and understanding of You. I Love You.

In Jesus' Name,

Amen

DAY 2

GOD HAS NOT FORGOT

2 Samuel 9:7 (KJV)

7 And David said unto him, Fear not: for I will surely show thee kindness for Jonathan, thy father's, sake and will restore thee all the land of Saul, thy father; and shall eat bread at my table continually.

Have you ever been in a place where you looked around and realized where you were was not where you were supposed to be? You felt out of place because you knew you deserved so much more than what you had received. And when you really thought about it, it was to no fault of your own. You are in a constant fight with depression, you are harming yourself, you can't stop crying, you are always angry, no healthy relationships, and you are in a very desolate place. But you know this isn't what God promised you, how did you get here? Maybe it was that abuse you endured as a child. Maybe you have suffered rejection. Are you still reliving those moments of abandonment? Whatever the reason, despite you being the victim, at one point in your life, GOD HAS NOT FORGOT!

In 2 Samuel, there is a young man by the name of Mephibosheth who was the grandson of King Saul and the son of Jonathan. After his father and grandfather were killed, his caretaker grabbed Mephibosheth and ran; but while fleeing, he was dropped and that made him handicapped. David and Mephibosheth's father, Jonathan, were friends; as a matter of fact, it was Jonathan who warned David that Saul wanted his life. Years later David is now King, and he asks if there is anyone in Saul's family still left and came to find that Mephibosheth was alive and lived in Lodebar, a very dry and desolate place. He sent for Mephibosheth and offered him a seat at his table for as long as he lived and assigned Mephibosheth his very own servants. It was because Mephibosheth was the grandson of a King and David had made a promise to Jonathan.

God did not forget Mephibosheth and he certainly will not forget you. Even though he was dropped and ended up in a very desolate place at no fault of his own, he still received what he was promised. Often times in life, we too have been dropped by others and find ourselves in a desolate place, mentally and emotionally, but God will find you right where you are and bring you to your promise. GOD HAS NOT FORGOT! Despite what has happened, you still have the right to a seat at the King's table.

~My Prayer~

Father God, thank You for showing me that where I am is not where I will stay. Everything that You have promised me will be mine. I know that You are a God that can meet me right where I am and bring me to where it is that You desire of me. No matter how bad it may seem, I find strength in knowing that You have not forgot. I no longer will fall victim to my past and the mistakes of others.

In Jesus' Name,

Amen

Day 3

ENLARGE MY TERRITORY

1 Chronicles 4:10 (KJV)

10 And Jabez called on the God of Israel, saying, oh that thou wouldest bless me indeed, and enlarge my coast, and that thine hand might be with me, and that thou wouldest keep me from evil, that it may not grieve me! And God granted him that which he requested.

1 Chronicles 4:10 speaks of Jabez, a man who we have all grown to know because of his prayer to God. Although Jabez was born into sorrow, he was a man who remained honorable in the sight of the Lord. Jabez prayed a powerful and faith filled prayer to God: "…Oh, that you would bless me and enlarge my territory! Keep your hand upon me, keep me free from evil, and remove any pain." Because Jabez remained faithful, God granted his request.

When Jabez prays this prayer in 1 Chronicles 4:10, he is asking that God be with him. He was not just asking God to bless him with things or just to see what he could get from God; his prayer was evidence of his faith and deep relationship with God. The boldness that Jabez demonstrated in his prayer is a good example for us to follow as we pray. Proverbs 28:1 says, "…the righteous are as bold as a lion." Like Jabez, we must be bold and declare out of our mouths the things that we are looking for God to do for us. We must know what we want and speak it. We must recognize that God is a sovereign God, that He cares for us, and that He is concerned.

Matthew 6:1-15 tells us that God desires a sincere and humble heart when we pray. The Lord's Prayer and the Prayer of Jabez are both perfect examples of how we should pray and seek God. Hebrews 4:16 says, " Let us therefore come boldly unto the throne of grace, that we may obtain mercy, and find grace to help in time of need." Bold prayers show us God's power!

Are you looking for God to enlarge your territory? Pray without hesitation, pray without boundaries, withholding nothing.

~My Prayer~

Father God, I thank You for hearing my prayers and enlarging my territory. Thank You for hearing my petitions and knowing what I stand in need of before I even ask. I pray that You would continue to shower me with Your love and blessings. Enlarge my territory. Keep Your hand on my life. Protect me from evil. I ask that You continue to show me mercy and grace in my time of need.

In Jesus' Name,

Amen

Day 4

IT'S AN INSIDE JOB

Psalm 51:10 (KJV)

10 Create in me a clean heart, O God; and renew a right spirit within me.

Though many of us fear change, change is often good. But what is it that makes one want to change? Is it the opinion of others? Is it how you feel about yourself? Is it guilt? No matter the desire for change, it is never too late. In our daily lives some of our actions are driven by self-gain, manipulation, arrogance, lust, or greed. We carry all these things in our heart, which ultimately impacts our actions and how we appear to others on the outside.

David was a noble man, yet he was not always this way. He was a sinner; he was self-indulgent. David's sins were followed one by another. His self-indulgence opened the door for lust, which eventually led him to murder. As the story goes, David saw a beautiful woman named Bathsheba bathing on a rooftop and requested that she be brought to him. Bathsheba, at the time, was married to Uriah. David indulged in a night of pleasure with the beautiful Bathsheba; he later received word from Bathsheba that she was pregnant. To cover his sin, David had to come up with a plan and that was to have Bathsheba's husband, Uriah, killed. David sent a letter to Joab ordering Joab to put Uriah on the front lines of the battle and have the other soldiers moved away from him so that he would be killed by enemy soldiers. After Uriah's death, David married the widowed Bathsheba. As a punishment from God for Uriah's murder and David's adultery, their first child died. David repented of his sins, and Bathsheba later gave birth to Solomon.

When we think of creation, we often think of something new. Something fresh. Something that only God can do. In this scripture David is the perfect example of a man after God's heart and earnestly desiring for change. After all his evil doing, he repented and realized that he needed to be cleansed from the inside out. He asked that God create in him a clean heart. As we can imagine in today's time, just like David, we are often overtaken by sin and worldly desires. We sometimes scheme and manipulate others to get what we want. We are often moved by our emotions and make unwise decisions. Like David, we should seek to ask God for a clean heart and a renewed spirit, a total makeover.

There may be some areas in your life today that are corrupt and sinful, but you do not have to stay there. Ask God today for a fresh start!

~My Prayer~

Father God, I pray now for purity. Create in a me a pure heart, a steadfast spirit of faithfulness and a willing spirit of service. Keep me from evil. Help me to not be moved by emotions, but to be led by your spirit. I pray for assurance that it is never too late, and to know that my past does not dictate my future. I thank you today for new beginnings.

In Jesus' Name,

Amen

Day 5

I SHALL LIVE AND NOT DIE

Psalm 118:17 (KJV)

17 I shall not die, but live, and declare the works of the Lord.

Persecution, trials, and tribulations are a part of life and all too common for some. There are days when you feel like the world is coming to an end, no one loves you, no one cares, and life is just not worth it anymore. The Bible gives us lots of assurance that trouble does not last always, that God is a shield and protector, and that He will supply all our needs. Yet in those desolate and trying times where we can't see God, we feel that all hope is lost. We want to give up, lay in bed all day, and throw in the towel. However, this is not God's will for our lives. Our outcomes are very much dependent upon how we react to situations.

In Psalm 118, we can imagine that the author has been going through some tough times and has thought about death or experienced close calls with death. He felt an imminent danger of dying. Throughout this Psalm he gives thanks for deliverance from his enemies. He saw that he was in danger. Circumstances around him did not look too good. People wanted to count him out and take his life. However, he had assurance that they would not win, they would not accomplish what they had set out to do. He knew that he would be protected and live to declare the goodness of the Lord. He declared that he would live and not die.

This is not uncommon today. When we experience negative things - sickness, depression, danger, or unrest - the mind tends to wander. Our first instinct is to go to the negative and to focus on all the what ifs. However, we should change our mindset. Our minds should be consumed with the thought and belief that we will be restored. Afterall, why should we doubt the hand of God on our lives?

What are you saying in times of turmoil and unrest? Are you saying, "I shall live and not die?" or are you saying that it is over for you. In the midst of bad situations, remain thankful and know that God is always there.

~My Prayer~

Father God, I thank you for life. Help me to speak life into my dead situations. Help me to see the good in things and rejoice in your goodness. I pray for peace, happiness, and joy in every area of my life. I cancel the assignment of the enemy when he tries to cloud my mind with thoughts that are not Your thoughts. I pray for healing from anxiety and depression. I pray that you release self-doubt and low self-esteem. I declare that I will prosper in whatever I do. I declare peace in every situation and area of my life.

In Jesus' Name,

Amen

Day 6

GODLY CONFIDENCE

Isaiah 54:17 (KJV)

17 No weapon that is formed against thee shall prosper; and every tongue that shall rise against thee in judgment thou shalt condemn. This is the heritage of the servants of the Lord, and their righteousness is of me, saith the Lord.

Often you can feel the weight of the world is on your shoulders. Everything that could happen, has happened. Those you love have stabbed you in the back. People are slandering your name. The doctor has given a bad diagnosis. The children are not acting right. Your marriage is falling apart. There is trouble on the job. All these situations are weapons that have formed to get you off track.

In this scripture, the prophet Isaiah speaks of weapons that form, but do not prosper. Every weapon that has been designed to destroy you, will destroy itself. Sometimes this means that the Lord takes the weapon from the hands of your enemies before they can even be used.

They may form the weapons, but they will not prosper. They may try, but they will fail. Sometimes He may allow the weapon to strike, but the outcome is much greater than the pain experienced. He says that the weapon will not prosper. You will not experience this forever.

Do you have this confidence in God? The confidence that you are protected. Confidence that He will remove the hand of your enemies or the tactics they are trying to use to destroy you? You serve a sovereign God, who has the power to protect: Criticism – Protected; Past hurts – Protected; Health concerns – Protected; Reputation – Protected. The Bible says that He knew you before you were formed in your mother's womb. This means He knows what will happen to you before it even happens. He has already paved the way and knows exactly how to protect you. You must remain confident and rest in Psalm 27: 1-3 – *"The Lord is my light and my salvation; whom shall I fear? the Lord is the strength of my life; of whom shall I be afraid? ² When the wicked, even mine enemies and my foes, came upon me to eat up my flesh, they stumbled and fell. ³ Though an host should encamp against me, my heart shall not fear: though war should rise against me, in this will I be confident."*

~My Prayer~

Father God, I thank you for protection. I thank you for removing the weapons from the hands of my enemies. Bless those who may try to form weapons against me. Bring them to the revelation of who You are and assure them that there is life in You. I pray that you would increase my confidence in You. I pray for a steadfast spirit so that I may stand in my times of persecution and when people turn their backs on me. Encamp your angels around me as I journey through life.

In Jesus' Name,

Amen

Day 7

IT'S ALREADY DONE

Philippians 4:19 (KJV)

19 But my God shall supply all your need according to his riches in glory by Christ Jesus.

Are you a giver and have a heart for giving to others, yet you always feel that your giving causes you to lack? God loves a cheerful giver and you can consider that whatever it is that you stand in need of is already done. Often, we desire to help and bless others, while we ourselves are in need. This is not uncommon, especially in the lives of givers. We always want to see everyone okay. We always give to others. Yet in the back of our minds we are left to wonder, "God, what about me?". What about me? What about my bills? What about food on my table? What about shelter? So many questions and we are struggling, yet we still want to give and make sure everyone else is okay, even when we are not.

In Philippians Chapter 4, Paul talks to the church about giving. This was a promise given by Paul to the church that had just sacrificially given to meet his need. The Philippians were the only church who gave to Paul when he was in need. His prayer and proclamation were that God would supply the needs of the people and bless them for being a blessing to him. Paul did not boast; however, he was thankful for his blessings and wanted others to receive the same in return. He states in Philippians 4:12, *"I know both how to be abased (what it is to be in need), and I know how to abound (to have plenty): everywhere and in all things I am instructed both to be full and to be hungry, both to abound and to suffer need."*

Have you learned to be content in all things or do you worry and try to figure it out on your own although God has already sent the message the He would supply all your needs? We can only imagine the worry, doubt, and fear that plagued the mind of the Philippian church, yet Paul gave them the assurance that just like they were a blessing to him, God was going to be a blessing to them. In other words, he was letting them know that it was already done, and that God would supply.

Bills past due…HE SHALL SUPPLY.

No food on the table…HE SHALL SUPPLY.

Eviction notice…HE SHALL SUPPLY.

Not enough money…HE SHALL SUPPLY.

Rest in God today, knowing that it is already done, and HE SHALL SUPPLY.

~My Prayer~

Thank you Lord for supplying all my needs according to Your riches. Your supply is generous! Your supply is blessed! Your supply is endless! I pray now for rest in Your ability to provide for me. I refuse to give up, worry, complain, or be stressed by what I see, knowing You will take care of me.

In Jesus' Name,

Amen

Day 8

ALL THINGS ARE POSSIBLE

Ephesians 3:20 (KJV)

20 Now unto him that is able to do exceedingly abundantly above all that we ask or think, according to the power that worketh in us.

Dreams and visions are things we have all experienced at one point in time. Some may seem beyond our reach or unrealistic. We may say to ourselves, certainly that is impossible. Yet, we can have those same dreams and visions for others and believe that it is possible for them. We become excited. We cheer them on. We stand in amazement of what they will accomplish.

That same amazement that we have in what others can do, is the same amazement or greater that we should have for what God can do. Why do we believe so much in others, but when it comes to God, we have limitations? He does not show up at the moment that we think we need Him, and we automatically think that our situation is too big for Him. In our minds we say, "God You said You could do it, but this situation is bigger than I ever imagined." Well, it may be bigger than you imagined, but it is not bigger than what God can do.

"Eye hath not seen, nor ear heard, neither have entered into the heart of man, the things which God hath prepared for them that love him." (1 Corinthians 2:9) This means that no one knows but Him. Think of things that you can comprehend, things that you have dreamed about, things that you have seen spiritually; well God is able to do far beyond that. The scripture says that He can do exceedingly, abundantly above all we can ask or think. That right there is enough to blow your mind. It is impossible for us to even comprehend so why try to figure it out. It is not in our strength.

We can waste so much time trying to figure God out and what will be His next move in our lives when we should just rest in who He is. Say to yourself, "I don't know what He is going to do, but I know that it is going to be BIG!!!"

~My Prayer~

Father God, I know that You are the God who specializes in the impossible. Blow my mind like only You can do. You say in Your word that You can do exceedingly, abundantly above all I could ever ask or think. Help my unbelief and show up and show out in every area of my life. For I know God that You live within me and that I can do all things through You. I do not have to worry, I do not have to fear because I know that Your power rests, rules, and abides within me. Help me to take the limits off you, God.

In Jesus' Name,

Amen

DAY 9

NEVER FORSAKEN

Matthew 28:20 (KJV)

20 Teaching them to observe all things whatsoever I have commanded you: and, lo, I am with you always, even unto the end of the world. Amen.

Have you ever felt alone and in a desolate place? Like no one quite understood how you felt or what you were going through. You begin to worry and feel as if even God himself has left you in your place of loneliness. Well you are not alone. God says that He is with us always, which means He will never leave us nor forsake us.

Jesus tells us that we should not worry about anything and that He is with us in all things. God will take care of our needs and even more just as He does for all of creation. He shines the sun on the just and the unjust. He loves us all even when we feel like He is not there. Jesus teaches us that the Kingdom of God is within us and that He lives within us. Once we see and know that we are in God and that God is in us it is impossible for us to believe that God has forsaken us.

Luke 15:11-32 tells us about the parable of the prodigal son. In this parable we see a father who has two sons. The younger son asks his father for his inheritance and the father grants his request. Upon receiving the inheritance, the younger son becomes wasteful and begins to live an extravagant lifestyle and eventually loses everything. After he has lost everything, the son is forced to return home with nothing. His plan is to ask his father to accept him as a servant; however, the father openly welcomes the son back and gives him above and beyond what he is expecting.

As we see in the parable of the prodigal son, even when we stray from the righteous path our Father is waiting to be reunited with us and restored in harmony. While we are traveling through our wilderness, being tested by the devil, God is there to see us through. The son was expecting to return as a servant, but his father, just like God our Father, still loved him unconditionally and desired to see him prosper. God wants His children to come back to Him; He will never forsake you and will welcome you back with open arms. No matter what you have done, you are not forsaken!! God protects His people. God provides for them. He did not bring you this far to leave you!!

~My Prayer~

Father God, I pray that You would continue to watch over me and provide for me. Even when it looks like I am lacking, I know that You will never leave me nor forsake me. I declare this day that I am blessed, that my children are blessed, that my children's children are blessed. I speak prosperity over my life and in the lives of those around me. Continue to prove Yourself to me Lord, and I will forever be grateful.

In Jesus' Name,

Amen

Day  10

GOD'S PLAN

Jeremiah 29:11 (KJV)

11 *For I know the thoughts that I think toward you, saith the* Lord, *thoughts of peace, and not of evil, to give you an expected end.*

God's plan for our lives can be likened to that of motherhood. A mother becomes pregnant and births a child, but even before the baby arrives, the mother is already making plans. She is planning what school the child will go to, what the child's room will look like, what sports or activities the child will engage in, and even what she wants for the child's future. The same way a mother has plans for her children, God has plans for us. Before we were formed in our mother's womb, God knew His thoughts towards us. He knew when, where, and how He would want to use us. He knew what our end would be. He knew that His desire for us was that we would prosper and be in good health. The good thing about God is that He will use whoever is a willing vessel to bring Him glory.

God will use the ones who we don't think can be used. He is preparing you in your mess. He will use your testimony to win others. You should not walk around in defeat nor look defeated because you have already been prepared by God for what's to come. What should have killed you didn't because of God's plan for your life. What should have overtaken you didn't work because God is going to use you for His glory. What should have taken your mind, God said no, I am not going to let that happen either. He is going to use all of it to bring you glory. Your family needs what is on your life. Don't you understand who you are!

Be reminded of what your mission and purpose is. Press into God with prayer. Your prayer life will sustain you. Be prepared to be used anywhere. You do not have to have a title. All He asks is that you know Him and surrender to His will for your life.

~My Prayer~

Father God, thank you for the plans for my life. Help me to relinquish control and to let You take charge. Help me to live a life of service and fulfill Your plan for my life. Even in those times where I feel like I am not qualified, help me to believe.

In Jesus' Name,

Amen

Day 11

I'M GOOD AT THE GATE

Acts 3:6-10 (KJV)

6 Then Peter said, silver and gold have I none; but such as I have given I thee: In the name of Jesus Christ of Nazareth rise up and walk. 7 And he took him by the right hand and lifted him up: and immediately his feet and ankle bones received strength. 8 And he leaping up stood, and walked, and entered with them into the temple, walking, and leaping, and praising God. 9 And all the people saw him walking and praising God. 10 And they knew that it was he which sat for alms at the Beautiful gate of the temple: and they were filled with wonder and amazement at that which had happened unto him.

Are you good with the Father? When there is chaos all around, do you still trust Him? Are you comfortable with just enough? Are you comfortable staying within the four walls and never reaching those on the outside or leading someone to Christ? Are you comfortable leaving people stuck in their situations although you have the power to help them out? Are you good at the gate?

Now is not the time to sit. We see what is going on in the world, in politics and in the church. Sometimes we can be so busy doing nothing, that the enemy is able to sneak in to push his agenda right under our nose. We do not walk in power and authority. We don't desire the power to work in us and through us. We are living in a day where we are powerless. We will ride pass the man on the street corner to get to church, because we can't miss prayer. Our cry is I'm good at the gate, I'm good doing what God has called me to do.

The man at the gate of Beautiful was laid at the gate every day to beg for alms and the prayer warriors just walked past him. Can you minister outside of the church? Can you do your assignment outside of the church? We are always supposed to ready and in position to minister to the broken.

This man is at the gate, his friends bring him every day, everyone passes him by. Peter and John come by. The man asks for money. Peter discerned his situation and asked the Lord what the root of his problem was. He didn't need money; he needed a touch from the Master. Peter said I don't have any money to give. Money will only fix it temporarily. If I give you Jesus, it will change your life forever.

If you have become comfortable in your situation, issue, and dysfunction God doesn't want you to stay in that place. He does not want you to be complacent. He does not want you to be good at the gate. He doesn't want you to let others get comfortable in being good at the gate. You are called to the ones that are messed up, the confused people, not just for Sunday morning. Your anointing is for everyone.

~My Prayer~

Father God, help me to not be good at the gate. I pray for courage to go outside of the four walls and to bring others to you. I pray for the boldness of a lion to approach people and meet them where they are. Let me not be so consumed with what I have going on but help me to be consumed with helping others and bringing them to the revelation of you.

In Jesus' Name,

Amen

Day  12

BE THE LIGHT

Matthew 5:14-16 (KJV)

14 Ye are the light of the world. A city that is set on a hill cannot be hid. 15 Neither do men light a candle, and put it under a bushel, but on a candlestick; and it giveth light unto all that are in the house. 16 Let your light so shine before men, that they may see your good works, and glorify your Father which is in heaven.

People are watching every move you make. If they never see God in the flesh, they are supposed to see God in you. A Christian should not let his light shine to be praised by others, but to bring glory to the Father. The Pharisees acted to be seen of men, but true Christians should behave to glorify God, caring little what people may think of them. It is by our conduct, that others may be brought into the likeness of God. We should live so that people may see God's way of life through our good works.

In the Parable of the Light recorded in Matthew 5:14-16, Jesus uses two metaphors to express our responsibility to influence the world: "a city on a hill" and "a lamp on a lampstand." Many Judean cities were established on the sides of mountains and travelers could see them from afar. Jesus pointed to such cities, telling His disciples that they were likened to them. Jesus' illustration of a shining lamp illuminating the home is the same influence that we should have in our homes, in our communities, and throughout the world. God's intention was that a Christian's actions should not be hidden from the eyes of neither our families or the world at large. Therefore, we must live a righteous, holy, humble, and pure life, letting our "light so shine before men and glorifying our Father in heaven."

Your upright life, pleasant attitude, and good works, including pure conversation and faithful obedience, should not be hidden but be seen and known. You cannot give light until you have received the grace of God and the Holy Spirit. Your life must produce the fruit of the Spirit, reflecting the shining example of Jesus Christ. It should always be evident in your community, in your business, at home and abroad, in prosperity and adversity.

Letting your examples shine requires that you resist the influence of the world. You cannot have a light that shines and at the same time live as the world does with its lust of the flesh, lust of the eyes, and pride of life (I John 2:16-17). Are you the light that shines amid a dark world?

~My Prayer~

Father God, I thank You for life. Thank You for placing me to be a light in the midst of a dark world. I pray that I will continue to be the one that brings peace in the midst of chaos, hope to the hopeless, and to encourage those who need encouragement. Bless me now. Keep me in perfect peace. Plant me in those places where I am needed the most so that men may see Your good works in me and glorify You.

In Jesus' Name,

Amen

Day 13

GIANTS DO FALL

Romans 8:28 (KJV)

28 And we know that all things work together for good to them that love God, to them who are called according to his purpose.

Life is full of ups and down, disappointments, heartbreaks and heartaches. These things are often seen as stumbling blocks or even giants that we just cannot seem to get around. God promises us that all things work together for the good for them that love Him. That means that God's powerful hand is required in our lives to transform bad to good; to destroy those giants.

This passage of scripture celebrates that God is always present and always willing to help in our hour of need; that, if God is for us, it really doesn't matter who is against us; and that there is no power strong enough or circumstance bad enough to separate us from the love of God.

It is in our dark times, our moments of weakness where God wants to display His glory.

We all suffer and experience hardship.

Some experiences are unbearable, and we want to know why we are suffering or if it is God Himself who has caused it. We question if He caused it, if He sympathizes, and if He can or will do anything about it. These are questions that many may have and that are common to the believer. Scripture does not say that God causes us to suffer nor does it say that God considers suffering to be a good thing. It says God works all things together for the good and for those who are called according to his purpose. Romans 8:18-39 is helpful for understanding our suffering as a Christian.

Know that God is with you in your suffering. He is not trying to punish you, but He is transforming you for His glory. Have faith in God when experiencing those giants in your life. Remind yourself that none of this is meant to destroy you, but that it is working for your good.

~My Prayer~

Father God, I trust your sovereignty. Whatever you do I will be satisfied. Fill me with Your anointing to withstand any situation. Help me to know and believe that the way out is to go through. I pray now for the strength to endure, the strength to stand strong, and the strength to press towards the mark. I pray for joy on the other side of through. I pray that You would restore the years I have sown in tears. Show me Your good, Lord and I will continue to bless Your name.

In Jesus' Name,

Amen

Day 14

I AM READY FOR OVERFLOW

1 Kings 18:41 (KJV)

41 And Elijah said unto Ahab, get thee up, eat and drink; for there is a sound of abundance of rain.

Have you ever had the feeling that something good is about to happen? You don't know what it is, but you know that God is up to something. You may experience this feeling, but when you do are you in a position to receive what God has in store for you. Are you ready for the overflow?

The children of Israel experienced a three-and-a-half-year drought in Samaria because of their disobedience and decision to turn their hearts away from God. They were in a dry land, thirsty, and malnourished. Elijah then receives a word from the Lord to go to tell Ahab that the rain is coming, but Ahab does not see a sign. Elijah takes Ahab to the top of the mountain and begins to call on the rain that the Lord already said was coming. He goes to the top of Mt. Caramel and begins to cry out to God. "Lord send your rain. Prove yourself again." He began to call on the rain before it was coming. He was ready for the overflow.

You may not see what is happening in the natural, but you may see it through the eyes of God. Be careful of sending people out to bring a report of what you already know God has given to you. Be careful who you listen to in this season. Elijah sent his servant out seven times to look for a sign and each time the servant came back with a negative report.

Even when it doesn't look like it, get ready. God sends the prophet Elijah to go back to these same people that turned their backs on Him so that He can prove Himself to them. If you repent, God will turn back your captivity and cause the rain to fall in your life again. He will free you to walk in power and the authority you are called to walk in. Like Elijah was ready for the rain (the blessing), we must also be ready for the rain (the overflow). You must make haste and ready for your affairs and be ready for what is to come.

The Bible says that the earth moans and groans and understands when something big is about to happen. Signs will be given. Something big is about to happen, and you must be prepared. You cannot be distracted by the drought but must stay in a position to receive.

~My Prayer~

Father God, thank you for loving me enough not to leave me where I am. Thank you for giving me time to make things right. Thank you for not leaving me in my mess. Break everything in me that is not like You so that I can be ready for the overflow in my life. Forgive me for all the times I have sinned against you. Don't let me stay in a place of bondage from where You are trying to free me. Rain on me so abundantly that I am strengthened supernaturally, physically, and financially.

In Jesus' Name,

Amen

Day 15

I BELONG HERE

Psalm 100:3 (KJV)

*3 Know ye that the L*ORD *he is God: it is he that hath made us, and not we ourselves; we are his people, and the sheep of his pasture.*

We must know that we belong to God and that we are His children, we are His heritage. We can often talk ourselves out of blessings by believing the reports and representations of others. We often walk by sight not by faith. Courage can only come from having a strong faith, which Caleb and Joshua alone possessed.

Numbers 13 talks about twelve men who were sent to search the land of Canaan, their instructions, what they did and their perception of the land. Numbers 13:33 says *"There we saw giants and we were in our own sight as grasshoppers."* When they looked at the men in the land of Canaan, they appeared to them as giants and the men immediately began to look at themselves and doubt.

God will send you to an environment to show you where you belong. You have what many need, but you must see yourself there. The 12 spies who were sent out came back and gave a report; 10 gave the negative, only two, Caleb and Joshua, believed they could possess the land. Because of their unbelief and because they did not see themselves there, the others had to stay in the wilderness another forty years. God showed them the possession. In the same way He is saying to us don't be afraid of the new season, new relationship, and new opportunities. Like the 10 men, we must get rid of the grasshopper mentality. Get rid of the woe is me mentality. Get rid of the victim mentality.

You are not a grasshopper, greater is He that is within you. No matter how big, wide, or large the situation appears – you belong here! If you don't see yourself as a giant, others won't see you that way. If you act like you don't belong, that's how people will treat you. Don't walk into seasons like you do not belong there. You are not a grasshopper; you belong there and must see yourself there. You must see yourself there because it is already yours. You must hold on to what the Lord says.

Stop saying you can't when God says you can. Stop saying you don't deserve it when God says you do. He is not giving it temporarily; He is giving it permanently. No one can take it away, it's yours because He wants you to have it. Sometimes our unbelief can overlook the promises and power of God, and magnifies every danger and difficulty, and makes us discouraged.

~My Prayer~

Thank you for reminding me that I belong in the promised land, in a place of joy, and in a place of prosperity. Forgive me for doubting and being afraid. God, I declare that I will not have any more missed opportunities or missed seasons because I felt unqualified or unworthy. Thank you for assuring me that I belong here. It is your will that I enter into the land of blessings. Thank you for establishing me in my new place for it is Your will that I do not struggle. God, help me to believe and find all things possible.

In Jesus' Name,

Amen

DAY 16

IT CANNOT BE DENIED

Acts 4:16 (KJV)

16 Saying, what shall we do to these men? for that indeed a notable miracle hath been done by them is manifest to all them that dwell in Jerusalem; and we cannot deny it.

People will often try to discredit the power of God that rests on your life. They will talk about your past, your current circumstances and even your future. They will try to count you out and doubt the change and the power of God that rests on your life. They will doubt your abilities and even doubt that you have the potential to change yourself or anyone else.

In Acts 4, we see Peter and John who face defiance because they were teaching that Jesus had risen from the dead and healed the lame man in the name of Jesus. The rulers, elders, and teachers of the law considered Peter and John to be blaspheming. They were greatly disturbed because the apostles were teaching the people, proclaiming in Jesus the resurrection of the dead.

They saw courage from ordinary men and were astonished although they couldn't explain what they were seeing. After witnessing the healing, they all noted that these men had been with Jesus. Their dilemma was that they could not punish the apostles for performing an act of compassion; yet if they did not stop these radicals, their status would be seriously threatened by the loss of followers. They ordered them not to speak or teach in the name of Jesus. They could not argue that a miracle had taken place because the healed beggar was standing right in front of them. The healing couldn't be denied.

Whenever you are doing something good, whenever you look like you are winning people will try to minimize what's on your life. There are some things that just cannot be denied and what cannot be denied is the power of God that rests on your life. What cannot be denied is the change that has taken place inside of you. They can talk about your past, but they cannot deny what God has done in your life right now. They can bring up things that may be on your record, but they can't deny what the Lord is doing in your life right now.

We are living in a season where God is releasing undeniable power and anointing upon us and there is nothing that will stand in the way of what He desires to do.

~My Prayer~

Father God, I thank you for working through me so that others may see Your power manifested through me. I pray for those that doubt Your power that reigns in my life. I pray that You would release Your power and anointing upon Your people and continue to perform miracles, signs, and wonders in my life.

In Jesus' Name,

Amen

Day 17

COMMAND IT

Romans 4:17 (KJV)

17 (As it is written, I have made thee a father of many nations,) before him whom he believed, even God, who quickened the dead, and calleth those things which be not as though they were.

When one thinks of commandments, they may think of giving direction, giving orders, and demanding that something be done at a specific time and place. Commandments are often birthed out of a desire to obtain a certain result. The Bible tells us that we must speak those things that are not as though they were. That means that we have the power to believe and speak things into existence.

When we look at the life of Abraham, he was the epitome of someone who had undeniable faith in God. God made something out of Abraham when he was a nobody. Scripture tells us that God set him up as a father to many nations. When everything was hopeless, Abraham believed anyway, deciding to live not based on what he saw he couldn't do but on what he knew God could do. He began to command things to happen in his life and thus began to see these things begin to happen.

Just like Abraham, we must learn to command our lives. He did not wait to see what was going to happen, but he spoke into his own life and commanded those things that God had already shown him. We must learn to be the voice in our own lives and to command our situations. Proverbs 18:21 tells us that death and life are in the power of the tongue. What are you speaking over your life? Start commanding your day!! Start commanding things to line up!!

Command what is dead to come back to life!!

Command the atmosphere to shift!!

Command your children to be saved!!

Command your life to line up with the Word of God!!

Command your business to prosper!!

Command your mind to be at peace!!

Command your body to be healed!!

Command your finances to increase!!

You don't ask you command!!

~My Prayer~

Father God, I come to You now thanking You for the strong faith to speak to my situations and to command that Your Word be fulfilled in my life. I speak now to every dry situation, every situation that does not look good, and everything in my life that is contrary to Your Word. I command healing in my body, I command financial blessings to overtake me, I command my mind to be at peace. I thank You for the manifestation of these things in my life. I thank You for increasing my faith to speak to my body, my mind, my household, and my family.

In Jesus' Name,

Amen

Day 18

DIG DEEPER

2 Kings 3:16-18 (KJV)

16 And he said, Thus saith the L ORD, Make this valley full of ditches. 17 For thus saith the L ORD, Ye shall not see wind, neither shall ye see rain; yet that valley shall be filled with water, that ye may drink, both ye, and your cattle, and your beasts. 18 And this is but a light thing in the sight of the L ORD: he will deliver the Moabites also into your hand.

In 2 Kings 3:11-20, we see three kings, the king of Israel, Jehoshaphat, and the King Edom who go to the prophet Elijah seeking help. Elijah is a prophet of the Lord and the king of Israel is a wicked king who came to consult Elijah. He was the son of Jezebel and Ahab, wicked people who did not honor God, but they worshipped Baal. Knowing this Elijah told the men to go seek counsel from the puppet prophets. The king of Israel refused and said to Elijah, it is your God that has dumped us kings into the hands of the Moabites. The kings are now in a very dry place, but because they were in the company of Jehoshaphat, Elijah agreed to help them.

Elijah commanded them to dig ditches all over the valley. He said you won't hear the wind or see the rain, but the valley will fill up with water. I need you to begin to dig ditches in your dry place. The valley is getting ready to be full of water. It is not just going to be enough for you, but also enough for those connected to you.

The three kings were in pursuit of their enemies the Moabites and banned together to go and take out their enemy. On their journey they get stuck. You may have started a journey but on your way, something happened that caused you to become stuck and lose your drive. God is saying it's time for you to dig. You put your shovel down because circumstances happened in the middle. That is where your trust and faith in God must kick in. You must trust God when you do not have all the details. While in pursuit the three kings walked into a famine, they went seven days with no food and no water. Have you ever been in a place where you felt dry, trapped, stuck, where you have lost your drive? For what God wants to do you can't continue to allow your present state to dictate how you respond. Don't let what is around define who you are.

Get your shovel out of the closet, it's time for you to dig. What you are asking is an easy thing for our God. He just needs you to start digging. That is, you saying God I trust you for the water. Digging is a sign of faith, a sign of confidence in the Lord.

~My Prayer~

Father God, thank You for being my peace. Thank You for being my strength. I love You. I pray for the strength to pick up my shovel and begin digging and preparing for what is to come. I thank You for handling everything that has stood in the way of my digging. Thank You for giving me a sweatless victory. Thank You for the power of obedience and the desire to dig again.

In Jesus' Name,

Amen

Day 19

NO MORE MISSED SEASONS

John 5:7 (KJV)

7 The impotent man answered him, Sir, I have no man, when the water is troubled, to put me into the pool: but while I am coming, another steppeth down before me.

Have you ever lost your fight and just become comfortable with your present circumstances? You see others flourishing in life and getting ahead of you, yet you are immobile, stuck in that same place for years and years? You come up with every excuse as to why you can't move, why you can't make that change, and why you can't jump ahead of others to get what's yours.

John 5:1-9 tells us about a man who lay lame at the Pool of Bethesda for 38 years. Like this man there were several others with infirmities who lay there waiting on the movement of the water. Verse 4 says that an angel went down at a certain season into the pool and troubled the water and whoever was the first to step in after the water was troubled was made whole of whatever disease he had. When Jesus saw the man lying there knowing that he had been there a long time, He asked if he wanted to be made whole. The man answered him, "Sir, I have no man, when the water is troubled, to put me into the pool: but while I am coming, another steppeth down before me."

This man was full of excuses. He was comfortable where he was and missed several opportunities to be healed of his infirmities. Can you imagine lying dormant for 38 years? You have missed opportunities to carry out what God has for you to do. You have missed out on enjoying life. You have become comfortable in your circumstances and missed so many seasons. That is the enemy's desire.

The enemy wants to make you tired. He wants to wear you out mentally. He wants you to think that you are not worthy of that opportunity or capable enough to go get it. He wants you to sit back and look at everyone else going ahead of you. God wants to know that you trust Him. You must be willing to leave the past and move forward. Don't you want more? Will you be made whole?

Instead of lying dormant and making excuses, use what you have gone through as a testimony that you survived, and it made you better. It hurt, but it was good for you. You can't stay stuck you've got to go higher. You must know that you are not who you were. God has done something new. Walk in newness now, walk in power now and let God do what He has already willed for you to do from the beginning. He has and will change your life. He will use you to minister to others. It was never about you; it was about the people you are called to minister to. What are you doing to allow the glory of God to be ministered through you? Are you missing opportunities? Are you missing your season to get what God has for you and to let God use you to bless others?

~My Prayer~

Father God, I pray now for no more missed seasons. I pray that You will not allow me to be complacent and satisfied in my current situation. I pray against the spirit of laziness and declare that I am made whole. I deserve everything you have for me and I qualify for the same blessings as others. I pray that you would lead me and guide me each day. Keep your hand upon my life, show me where to go and what to do to bring you glory.

In Jesus' Name,

Amen

Day 20

SET BACK FOR A SETUP

Job 42: 10,12,16-17 (KJV)

10 And the Lord turned the captivity of Job, when he prayed for his friends: also, the Lord gave Job twice as much as he had before. 12 So the Lord blessed the latter end of Job more than his beginning: 16 After this lived Job a hundred and forty years, and saw his sons, and his sons' sons, even four generations. 17 So Job died, being old and full of days.

We all know the story of Job. When we struggle, it is often hard to understand. We question if God is truly God, how can He allow such bad things to happen. The book of Job gives those who suffer encouragement by showing that true godliness is shown during suffering and what happens after we come out of our suffering.

Job is a wealthy man who lives in the land called Uz. He has been blessed with a large family, ten children, and thousands of flocks. To his friends and those around him, Job is known to live a blameless and upright life and is one who avoids evil at all costs. One day, Satan appears before the Lord. The Lord is speaking to Satan about Job's uprightness and godliness. Satan argues that Job is only this way because of all the things he has been blessed with. Satan tells God that if Job is punished, he will surely turn and curse God.

God allows Satan to torment Job, to test him with one stipulation – Satan can't take Job's life in the process. In the course of one day, Job loses his livestock, servants, and ten children. Job tears his clothes and shaves his head in mourning, but he still blesses God. Satan appears to God again, and God allows him another chance to test Job. This time, Job is afflicted with horrible skin sores. His wife, the one closest to him, encourages him to curse God, to give up and die, but Job refuses. He refuses to accept his circumstances and continues to trust God. He boldly declares that he knows his Redeemer lives.

Job is robbed of every sign of God's favor on his life. He lost everything. In the end, everyone is silenced – the adversary, Job's friends, and Job himself – but not God. Job was a modest man, he never cursed God. God gave him double for his trouble. The Bible says that *the LORD BLESSED THE LATTER END OF JOB MORE THAN HIS BEGINNING.* What do you do when you have lost everything? Do you throw in the towel and curse God? Or do you know that it is just a setup by God? Do not allow others to talk you out of your blessing but stand firm on who you know God to be to you. Know that Satan cannot touch you without God's permission; so, know if you are facing affliction God has allowed it, but it is only a setback for a setup.

~My Prayer~

Father God, thank You for my setbacks. Thank You for the times where I felt like everything was going wrong and I felt like I was going to die in it. Thank You for showing me that my latter will be greater than my past. I pray for a steadfast spirit so that I may continue to endure my setbacks for they are working something much greater on the inside of me. Bless me Lord. Keep me under Your wings and continue to help me stand in the face of adversity.

In Jesus' Name,

Amen

Day 21

TRANSFORMED BY HIS GLORY

2 Corinthians 3:18 (KJV)

¹⁸ But we all, with open face beholding as in a glass the glory of the Lord, are changed into the same image from glory to glory, even as by the Spirit of the Lord.

The word transformed means to change into another form. It is likened to the process of a caterpillar changing into a butterfly.

In Acts 8, you have a man, Saul, who persecuted Christians, he hated anyone who named the name of Jesus. He had a bad past, he was angry, he was a killer, everyone was afraid to be in his presence. But there was still something special about him. It was the hand of God that was still on his life. Not matter how messed up he was, God still had a plan for him. Saul was on his way to Damascus with a letter from the high priest of the temple in Jerusalem giving him authority to arrest anyone who followed Christ. While on the Damascus road a bright light shined on Saul, causing his entire party to fall to the ground. Jesus appeared to Saul asking, "Why are you persecuting me?" in a voice only understood by Saul. Saul was speechless and asked what Jesus wanted him to do. Jesus tells him to rise and go to Damascus where he would be told what to do. Even though Saul received his commission from Jesus on the road, he still had to go into Damascus and be told what to do—meet with Ananias who laid hands on him, receive the Holy Spirit, be baptized, and be received by the disciples there.

When we think of the Damascus Road Experience we think about a dramatic transformation. Similarly, many people may receive Christ in this manner, while others' transformation may be more of a gradual process. Jesus made it clear to Saul that he had done it his way long enough. It was now time for transformation and to be used by God to do His will.

This is the same transformation that Christians likewise should go through. We should not just talk about the power of God; we should show some signs. We must come with power and demonstration to change lives. Romans 12:1 says "Be ye transformed by the renewing of your mind so that we may prove that what is good, perfect and the acceptable will of God."

We all need a change. We need to be transformed by the glory of God. If we are not transformed, we will mess up some things. God wants to do something in you. When you become Christlike, you will get Christlike results. Allow God to control you, He can do so much with you. There is work for you to do, people are assigned to you. Get in order with His will and assignment so that you can be used for His glory.

So often we ask God to send His glory and to show us His glory, but we must understand what the glory really is. We are to walk in the light, others should know that we are saved. When the real glory comes, no flesh can glory. Yokes are broken, you want to make wrongs right, the glory comes to give you direction, to transform your life. We must be partakers of His image. When He looks at us, He should see Himself. God wants you to look like Him so that you can represent Him. The glory comes to transform your life into His divine nature. He comes to do a new thing in you.

~My Prayer~

Father God, send Your glory so that I may be a witness to others of who You are. Continue to do a new thing in me. Show me Your ways God. Help me to walk upright so that it is evident that Your glory rests upon me. You changed my life so that I could be free and walk in freedom. Thank You for my change.

In Jesus' Name,

Amen

Day 22

I AM WHAT YOU SEE

Ephesians 1:4 (KJV)

⁴ According as he hath chosen us in him before the foundation of the world, that we should be holy and without blame before him in love (in His sight).

Many of us find ourselves defining our self-worth based on how others see us and on our accomplishments, feeling shame from our past, defining our value based on our looks, or setting unrealistic standards for ourselves. But it doesn't have to be this way. If only we could see ourselves as God sees us! Our identity is found in Jesus Christ. It is rooted in His grace and mercy. Our identity is that of a child of God and a joint heir with Jesus Christ. Scripture tells us that we are made in the image of God. How we see ourselves is our perception.

Perception is what you think. It is what you think you saw. What you think you sense. As a Christian, what do you see when you see yourself? What do you perceive, what is your perception of yourself? Do you see yourself a chosen vessel? Do you see yourself as a child of God? Do you see yourself as God sees you?

The Bible tells us in 1 Peter 2:9 that *"You are a chosen people, a royal priesthood, a holy nation, a people belonging to God, that you may declare the praises of him who called you out of darkness into his wonderful light."* It also says in Matthew 5:13-16 that we are the salt of the earth, and a light in a dark world. Salt preserves, cleanses, purifies, heals, and restores. Do you know that you are called to be the answer? When God looks at you, can He see your light? Is it evident that you are the salt of the Earth? Do you even see yourself this way?

Today, decide to see yourself victorious! See yourself healed! See yourself free! See yourself faithful! See yourself at peace! See yourself rejoicing! See yourself as the lender not the borrower! See yourself as the head and not the tail! See yourself above and not beneath!

~My Prayer~

Father God, help me to see myself the way that you see me. In my moments of pain, help me to see myself healed. In my moments of weakness, help me to see myself strong. In my moments of sorrow, help me to see myself happy. In my moments of distress, help me to see myself at peace. Help me to believe I am what you see.

In Jesus' Name,

Amen

Day 23

THE FIGHT IS FIXED

Ephesians 6:10-12 (KJV)

10 Finally, my brethren, be strong in the Lord, and in the power of his might. 11 Put on the whole armor of God, that ye may be able to stand against the wiles of the devil. 12 For we wrestle not against flesh and blood, but against principalities, against powers, against the rulers of the darkness of this world, against spiritual wickedness in high places.

Some are all too familiar with professional wrestling. When watching, we see people hitting each other over the head with chairs, we see heroic acts, and from time to time we may even see some blood, or someone being injured. It is perceived by many that these fights are rigged by the promoters to make more money and build the anticipation of the crowd. Fixing the fight raises the stakes.

Unlike professional wrestling, in the Christian world, the Bible tells us that we do not wrestle against flesh and blood, but our fight is still fixed. We are already predestined to win. Ephesians 6:13–18 tells us that we are to stand firm with our loins (waist) girted with truth, the breastplate of righteousness, the gospel of peace, the shield of faith, the helmet of salvation, the sword of the Spirit, and by always praying in the Spirit. This means that we are to know the truth, believe the truth, and speak the truth. We are to rest in the fact that God has already sacrificed for us and that the fight is already fixed. We should not be afraid, become timid, waiver in our faith, or throw in the towel no matter how great the attack because the fight is fixed. Our ultimate defense is the assurance we have of our salvation, which no man can take away. We have prayer, we have the Word of God. We can only stand strong in the Lord's power, it is God's armor that protects us, and our battle is ultimately against spiritual forces of evil in the world. What are you wrestling with today?

Jesus is our ultimate example of resisting temptation in spiritual warfare. Recall how Jesus handled direct attacks from Satan when He was tempted in the wilderness (Matthew 4:1–11). The Bible, God's Word, is the most powerful weapon that we must use to stand against the wiles of the devil. It tells us to hide His words in our hearts. The word that can be used in times of affliction and in times of uncertainty. This word gives us peace and assures us that the fight is already fixed.

Today, seek to rely on the power of God and not to operate in your own strength. Put on the whole armor of God. Talk to God through prayer. Read the Bible. Stand firm. Submit to the will of God for your life. The fight is fixed!!!

~My Prayer~

Father God, I thank You for protection. Thank You for being my shield, my fortress, my rock, a very present help in the time of trouble. Thank You for Your Word that keeps me going in the midst of my troubles. God, help me to believe that the battle is not mine, but that it is Yours and that You have already fixed the fight. You have already predestined me to win.

In Jesus' Name,

Amen

Day 24

FAITH – FORSAKING ALL I TRUST HIM

Hebrews 11:1 (KJV)

***11** Now faith is the substance of things hoped for, the evidence of things not seen.*

Faith over fear is something we commonly hear as Christians. We are often taught to put our faith into action and to trust God in all things. We are told not to be scared, not to grow weary, but instead to trust where God is taking us to even when we can't see what He is doing or where He is taking us.

To have faith is to have a strong belief in something or to put your trust and confidence in someone. As a Christian, you are supposed to have faith in God. The Bible says, *"Now faith is the substance of things hoped for, the evidence of things not seen."* (Hebrews 11:1). Faith is the main ingredient that we as Christians should have when in a relationship with God. Faith is a strong belief that God's words are true, and that God will perform all that He has promised.

When you think of faith in the Bible, Abraham is probably one of the first people who comes to mind. Romans 4:3 tells us, *"Abraham believed God, and it was counted unto him for righteousness."* When speaking of Abraham, Romans 4:18-21 says *"Who against hope believed in hope, that he might become the father of many nations, according to that which was spoken, so shall thy seed be. And being not weak in faith, he considered not his own body now dead, when he was about an hundred years old, neither yet the deadness of Sarah's womb: He staggered not at the promise of God through unbelief; but was strong in faith, giving glory to God; And being fully persuaded that, what he had promised, he was able also to perform."*

Abraham was old in age, which means at this time he had most likely seen and endured a lot in his lifetime, but that did not deter his faith. He was strong in faith. Abraham simply believed that God would do what He said. Hebrews 11:8 tells us, *"By faith Abraham obeyed when he was called to go out to the place which he would receive as an inheritance. And he went out, not knowing where he was going."* Abraham had no idea where he was going, but he trusted God that much to go ahead and depart. He trusted and believed God that He would guide him and his family along the way. There was no questioning, no pondering, no convincing himself and no waiting. He moved immediately! He showed his faith by departing. Like Abraham we see that we must demonstrate our faith by being obedient to God.

Today, believe that God can do the impossible and that nothing is too hard for God. Believe in God's power and promises, without wavering. Believe and be willingly obedient to God.

Trust God's guidance and direction in leading you into uncharted territory. Nothing is too hard for God. Nothing is impossible for God.

~My Prayer~

Father God, I thank You for faith. I thank You for providing me with direction for what You have for me next. I may not know where I am going, but I trust You to lead the way. I pray that You would strengthen my faith. Give me the faith of Abraham to move when You say move without any questions. I pray for courage to get up and go and to leave that which is familiar behind. I thank You for my new place! I thank you for erasing any fear and doubt that may try to creep in and overtake my faith in you, God. I declare it already done!!

In Jesus' Name,

Amen

Day 25

ACCESS GRANTED

Hebrews 4:16 (KJV)

16 Let us therefore come boldly unto the throne of grace, that we may obtain mercy, and find grace to help in time of need.

When we think of celebrities or people with an elite status, we know that we must go through all kinds of protocols and security clearances to gain access to them. We do not have to do this to get to God. We do not have to wait in a line to access God. We do not have to go through a background check. We do not have to have a special code to get in. Access has already been granted anytime and anywhere. God just asks that you call on Him in prayer.

According to the Bible, prayer is a method of interacting with God in a personal manner. When we go to God in prayer, we are thanking Him for who He is, what He has done, and petitioning him for our requests. Perfect examples of those who prayed to access God in the time of trouble are Moses, Job, and even Jesus in the Garden of Gethsemane.

Peter tells us in 1 Peter, that we have the right, privilege, and responsibility to go directly to God. We can pray and talk to God, worship, and fellowship with God. Philippians 4:6 says, *"Be careful for nothing; but in everything by prayer and supplication with thanksgiving let your requests be made known unto God."* Access to the Father is made possible through Jesus.

Recall when Jesus died on the cross, there was a veil in the temple that separated where God's Spirit was, from where man was. Only priests could go behind the veil once a year. When Jesus died on the cross, God ripped that veil from top to bottom, symbolizing that there was no longer a barrier. We now had access!!

You now have direct access to God. You don't have to pray through anybody else. You don't have to confess through anybody else. You don't have to fellowship with God through anybody else. Read your Bible, talk with the Lord, and fellowship directly with Him.

~My Prayer~

Father God, thank You for the gift of prayer and access to You. Thank You for hearing my petitions when I come before You in prayer. I am forever grateful for unlimited access. Help me to call out to You in times of trouble and not to rely on others. Give me the words to say when I feel like I do not know how to pray. Continue to show Your love, grace and mercy towards me.

In Jesus Name,

Amen

DAY 26

BE BOLD – JUST DO IT!!

Ephesians 3:12 (KJV)

***12** In whom we have boldness and access with confidence by the faith of him.*

Whether you are shy or outgoing, introvert or extrovert, being bold is something that we all struggle with, especially when chartering unfamiliar territory or situations. When one is bold, they lack fear. Being bold means that you are willing to do something despite what may happen or what people may say. When making a bold move, you have already considered that you do not know what the outcome may be. It may be good or bad; you may be embarrassed or even humiliated in the process. This can involve things as simple as praying at church in front of the congregation, delivering a speech, introducing yourself to someone new, asking someone on a date, or even trying to approach your favorite celebrity. There is an unknown outcome in all these situations. It can go well, or it can go bad.

Part of being bold is being open and saying "yes" to unfamiliar things that are presented to you; however, in saying "yes" there must be boundaries. Boldness is acting, by the power of the Holy Spirit, in the face of some threat or an adverse outcome. To be bold you must be empowered by the spirit, have courage, and have urgency. If one or the other is missing, you won't act boldly. Without conviction that something should be said or done, what's there to be bold about? Without courage, you will have a hard time facing opposition or threats. Without a sense of urgency, we lack the drive and motivation to make that step.

We as Christians today and even the early church didn't always feel bold. In Acts 4, when the disciples returned, they told the others of the threats of persecution and possible execution that they were receiving. Though they were being threatened, they did not run. They did not go into hiding. Instead, they prayed for boldness: *"And now, Lord, behold their threatenings: and grant unto thy servants, that with all boldness they may speak thy word, By stretching forth thine hand to heal; and that signs and wonders may be done by the name of thy holy child Jesus. And when they had prayed, the place was shaken where they were assembled together; and they were all filled with the Holy Ghost, and they spake the word of God with boldness."* (Acts 4:29-31) As they prayed, their fear melted away and they received a fresh filling of the Holy Spirit and renewed boldness to keep speaking.

Is there something you've always wanted to do, but avoid it because it's out of your comfort zone? That's a clear sign you should consider doing it even if it is uncomfortable. Today, do one thing that's out of your comfort zone just to see what happens. Afterall, what do you have to lose?

~My Prayer~

Father God, I pray now for boldness. I pray for the courage to do those things that have been holding me back. No matter the outcome, I trust You and know that You will not lead me to a place of danger. Whatever it takes, release the fear that has held me bound and increase my boldness to do Your works and to share the good news of the gospel with others.

In Jesus' Name,

Amen

Day 27

NOT GUILTY

Romans 8:1 (KJV)

8 There is therefore now no condemnation to them which are in Christ Jesus, who walk not after the flesh, but after the Spirit.

Not guilty means to be innocent. It means an acquittal from a wrongdoing. What is guilt? It is a *feeling* of doing something wrong or going against standards, rules, or laws. It can involve cultural issues, family issues, legal issues and especially sins related to violating God's standards. Also, guilt can come from feelings of inadequacy due to not living up to your own standards. Guilt does not have to involve horrible sins but can include feelings of being unworthy of God's love simply because of a multitude of minor wrongdoings. When one feels guilty or is guilty, the first reaction is to run and hide or try to cover the sin, but you cannot hide from yourself and you cannot hide from God.

1 John 1:9 says, *"If we confess our sins, he is faithful and just to forgive us our sins and to cleanse us from all unrighteousness."* Psalm 103:10-14 lets us know that *"He has not punished us as we deserve for all our sins, for His mercy towards those who fear and honor Him is as great as the height of the heavens above the earth."* In Matthew 18:22, Jesus says that church members should forgive each other *"seventy times seven times"*, a number that symbolizes no boundaries. One of the most celebrated forgiveness texts is Jesus' prayer from the cross, *"Father, forgive them; for they do not know what they are doing"* (Luke 23:34). Through our relationship with Christ our sins are forgiven, and we are secured.

If we wish to be free of guilt, we need to deal with it honestly and openly. Confession means to say the same thing about your sin that God says about it. It means that you don't dummy it down, you don't just throw it out the window. You call your sin exactly what God calls it. The Bible says that if you confess your sins, He is faithful and just to forgive us. God's Son died on a cross for you to experience forgiveness. If forgiveness was not important, there is no way Jesus would have suffered as He did. Sin and guilt are serious issues. We cannot be healthy and happy while living with guilt. God knew that and made a provision for us to be free of guilt. He does not just save us in order that we can go to heaven; He saves you to have life and to have it more abundantly.

When most people sin, they begin to feel guilty. We all have sin; therefore, we all deal with the spirit of guilt. Don't put yourself down. Don't count yourself out. Don't give up! Your case went into heaven, you had a good lawyer. God was crucified for your sins and you're – NOT GUILTY.

~My Prayer~

Father God, thank You for saving me from the guilt of sin. Thank You for the paving the way for my path to righteousness. In those times where I feel guilty, help me to believe that You died for my sins and all I have to do is confess and You will forgive me. I pray that I will not continue to live in nor be bound by my past mistakes. Continue to keep me on the right path that I may live in obedience to Your word.

In Jesus' Name,

Amen

Day

28

REAL LOVE

1 Peter 4:8 (KJV)

8 And above all things have fervent charity (love) among yourselves: for charity (love) shall cover the multitude of sins.

If you grew up in the church, then you have more than likely heard someone say that love covers a multitude of sins. But how often do we apply this scripture in our daily lives. We hold grudges, we are quick not to forgive others, and we even count others out when they have done wrong or made a mistake. This is not God's desire for His children and does not exemplify unconditional love.

Wondering what unconditional love looks like? Well, it is to love someone unselfishly, despite circumstances and showing that you care about the happiness of the other person and will do anything to help them despite what you may or may not get in return. In other words, love without conditions. Love without limitations. When dealing with others, we can often become judgmental and forget to seek and give that same love that God so freely gives us. The Bible tells us that God is love. He created us and saved us from our sins. Romans 5:8 says, *"But God shows his love for us in that while we were still sinners, Christ died for us."* John 15:13 says, *"Greater love hath no man than this, that a man lay down his life for his friends."* 1 John 4:8 says, *"He that loveth not knoweth not God; for God is love."* These are the perfect examples of unconditional love.

The greatest power known to man is that of unconditional love. When we allow ourselves to understand the impact our actions have not only on ourselves but on others, we realize how important it is to love others in their mess. We each have the power to wrong the rights, to forgive, to move on, and to love unconditionally.

Today be intentional and practice random acts of kindness. Reach out to someone who you may have misjudged. Forgive those who you feel have wronged you or treated you inappropriately. Forgiveness is the easiest and most powerful act of kindness you can do both for yourself and for others. When you realize your potential to love unconditionally, you become a new person and can in turn positively impact the lives of others.

~My Prayer~

Father God, thank You for your love. Thank You for showing me what love is. I ask that You show me how to love unconditionally. Cleanse my heart Lord so that I may not judge others. Help me to understand what others may be going through. I pray for the courage to reach out to those who have wronged me, the courage to reconcile broken relationships, the courage to do something nice for someone in need, and the courage to love despite circumstances. Help me to love like You Lord.

In Jesus' Name,

Amen

Day 29

THE POWER OF PATIENCE

Galatians 6:9 (KJV)

9 And let us not be weary in well doing: for in due season we shall reap, if we faint not.

Today's generation is what we may call the microwave generation. We do not like waiting, we want to be obtain things quick, fast, and in a hurry. We are constantly on the go. We like fast service, fast results, fast food, fast relationships, and fast money. We want to get to our destinations quickly. When things are moving too slow and not happening fast enough, we grow very impatient. We want to go against what is godly to speed things up and we want others to suffer for not doing and giving us what we want when we want it. Patience is often viewed as a negative thing because we feel we are suffering in the wait. The Bible teaches us that God is patient. We are supposed to be patient with everyone around us. When we envision patience, we can imagine someone waiting calmly without complaining. They are calm, they are at rest. According to the dictionary, the common definition of patience is "the capacity to accept or tolerate delay, trouble, or suffering without getting angry or upset."

In Acts 10 the Bible talks about Cornelius, who was a Gentile who believed in God. He lived a life that exemplified a deep faith in God. Because of his faith, God sent an angel to speak to him and to tell him to send men to Joppa to get Peter and to bring him back to his house. Cornelius did as instructed. While God was speaking to Cornelius, Peter was on the roof of his house praying. The men from Cornelius' house then showed up and Peter went down to meet them after which the men, Peter and some of Peter's men, left to go to Cornelius' house. When Peter and the men arrived, the house was full of people waiting to see Peter. Peter preached the gospel of salvation and everyone in the house believed and was saved by God.

In the account of Cornelius, we see a man who had patience enough to follow what God said to do even though there was no mention as to why he was to send men to get Peter. Without knowing even if Peter would come, he called his family and friends to his house to wait for Peter. The result of this was that everyone who had patience with Cornelius to wait and see what would happen were saved. This teaches us that we not only must have patience with God, but also have patience with each other (Romans 12:10-21). We also learn that not having patience can sometimes have long lasting effects for many generations (Isaiah 30:15-18).

When we go through times of testing, we often do not see why God allowed it to happen until many years later when we can look back and understand exactly why God allowed it. (Ecclesiastes 7:7-10). God requires that we live a life of patience, patiently waiting for the promises of God to be fulfilled.

Today make patience your goal for the entire day. Make an intentional effort to take your time and think about everything you do, be mindful and live in the moment. Slow down. Being patient allows you time to think and evaluate what is going on around you. You can make better decisions. As you continue to pray and seek God, He will show you how He uses your patience for your good and for His glory.

You must let the Lord know you don't mind waiting. Isaiah 40:31 says *"But they that wait upon the LORD shall renew their strength; they shall mount up with wings as eagles; they shall run, and not be weary; and they shall walk, and not faint."* The closer you draw to God the more you will find that patience is so necessary in the life of a Christian.

~My Prayer~

Father God, I pray today for patience. I pray for a spirit of longsuffering. Help me to slow down and to let You work like only You can. In my season of waiting, prepare me for what is to come. Teach me to be still because Your timing is always perfect. Help me to trust Your timing, Lord. Help me to surrender to Your plan. Help me to stand still and see Your works.

In Jesus' Name,

Amen

Day 30

A HEART TO WORSHIP

John 4:23-24 (KJV)

23 But the hour cometh, and now is, when the true worshippers shall worship the Father in spirit and in truth: for the Father seeketh such to worship him. 24 God is a Spirit: and they that worship him must worship him in spirit and in truth.

One cannot have a true relationship with God without having a heart for worship. To worship God means to honor Him and to give reverence to Him for who He is and what He has done.

Worship is essential to a Christian's faith. Christians must worship God to thank Him for his love, ask for forgiveness for their sins, and to understand His will for their lives. To ensure we stay in a posture of worship, we must keep God at the forefront of our minds. David spoke of this when he wrote, "*I have set the* Lord *always before me: because he is at my right hand, I shall not be moved. Therefore, my heart is glad, and my glory rejoiceth: my flesh also shall rest in hope."* (Psalm 16:8-9)

As we go through life and get busy, our hearts must still grow close to God through worship. We must keep Him in our hearts and obey Him in everything we do. Therefore, worship is so important; in worship we quiet ourselves before God.

John 4:23 says, *"But the hour cometh, and now is, when the true worshippers shall worship the Father in spirit and in truth: for the Father seeketh such to worship him."* We worship God because of who He is, because of his divine nature, because He is a good God, because of the things that He does for us each day. When we approach God, we must approach Him in spirit. The place, the time, words, music, dances, postures, and sounds, and all other outward things are important because they can rid the distractions from the outside world and can lift our spirit man; however, the moment they act as a distraction they hinder true worship. Having a sincere heart is required for worship. God wants us to worship with a sincere soul, heart and mind. To worship in truth is in harmony with the nature God. A true worshipper is in accordance with the divine will of the Father. God desires our worship. He desires that those who worship Him would worship Him in spirit and in truth. God is not a fleshly Being, but He is a spiritual Being, and requires a worship that is proportionate to His Being; therefore, those that worship Him, must do it with their spirits and in truth.

Worship breaks chains! Worship exalts God! Worship causes us to love God more than others! Worship causes the atmosphere to shift! There are several ways to worship God today. This can be done in music and speech, reading the scripture, praying, or preaching a sermon to name a few.

Today, change your posture to a posture of worship. Start your day by worshipping God for who He is. Think on the goodness of the Lord and mediate on it throughout the day. Get a song of worship in your heart that shows God how you feel about Him and how grateful you are.

~My Prayer~

Father God, I pray now for a heart of worship. I pray that You would remove all distractions so that I may worship You in spirit and in truth. I pray that You would open my heart and mind for worship. I pray that You would bring to my remembrance who You are to me and what You have done for me. I pray for a lifestyle of worship. I pray that worship will be my portion as I go about my day. I thank You. I love You. I trust You.

In Jesus' Name,

Amen

www.ingramcontent.com/pod-product-compliance
Lightning Source LLC
Chambersburg PA
CBHW021118080526
44587CB00010B/563